WORLD
RELIGIONS

Written by Brian Doyle
Illustrated by Derry Dillon

Published 2018
Poolbeg Press Ltd

123 Grange Hill, Baldoyle
Dublin 13, Ireland

Text **and illustrations** © Poolbeg Press Ltd 2018

A catalogue record for this book is available from the British Library.

2

ISBN 978 1 78199 833 5

All rights reserved. No part of this publication may be reproduced or transmitted in any form or by any means, electronic or mechanical, including photography, recording, or any information storage or retrieval system, without permission in writing from the publisher. The book is sold subject to the condition that it shall not, by way of trade or otherwise, be lent, resold or otherwise circulated without the publisher's prior consent in any form of binding or cover other than that in which it is published and without a similar condition, including this condition, being imposed on the subsequent purchaser.

Cover design and illustrations by Derry Dillon
Printed by **L&C Group, Poland.**

A World of Religions . . .

There are thousands of religions in the world. All are paths human beings follow to live good lives, and to reach out to the eternal spirit we call 'God'. However, religions differ in what exactly they imagine this spirit to be and how we human beings can become one with it.

In this book we take a look at six of the largest religions in the world and learn what they have in common, so that hopefully we may all understand each other and learn to live in peace, side by side.

BUDDHISM
CHRISTIANITY
HINDUISM
ISLAM
JUDAISM
SIKHISM

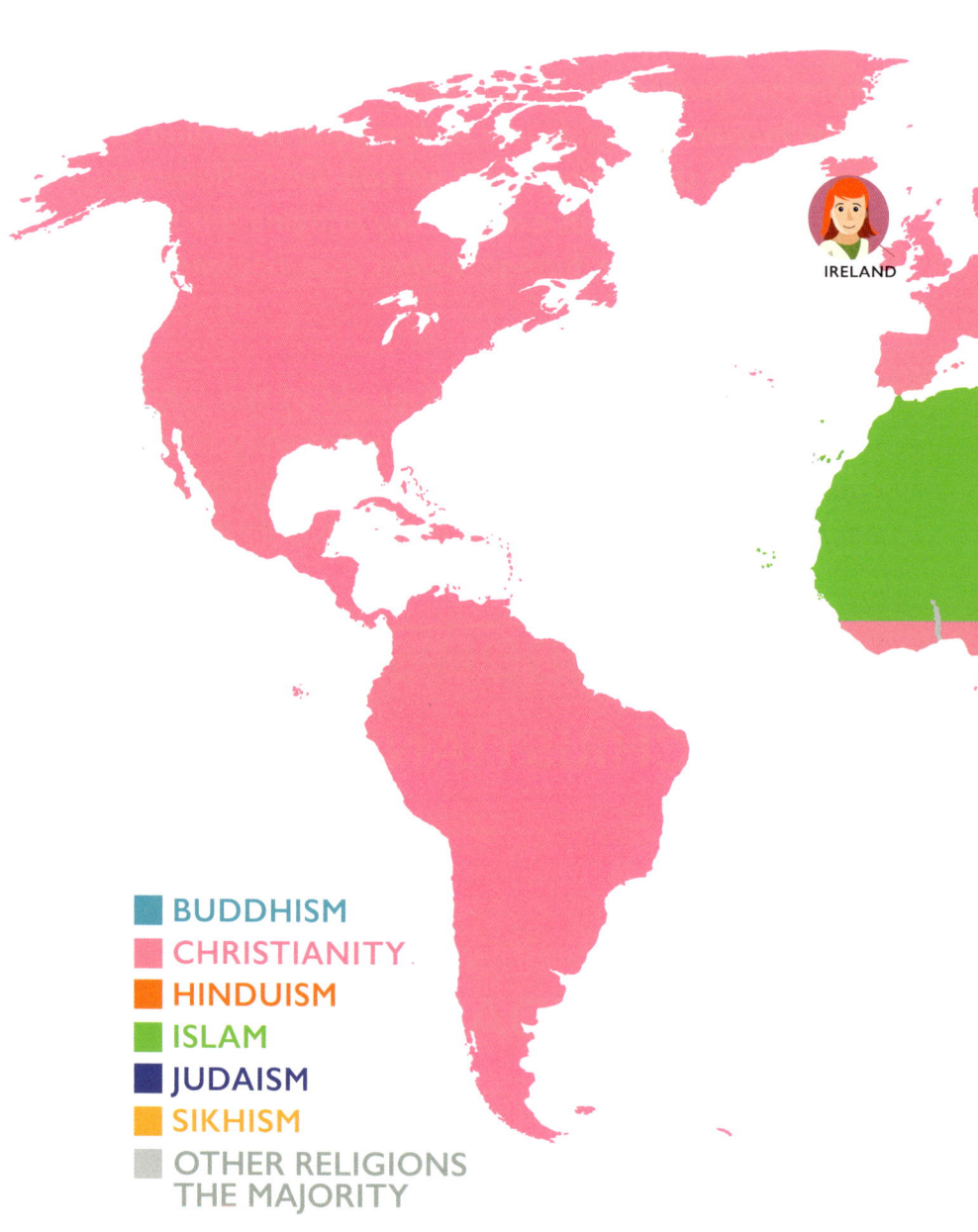

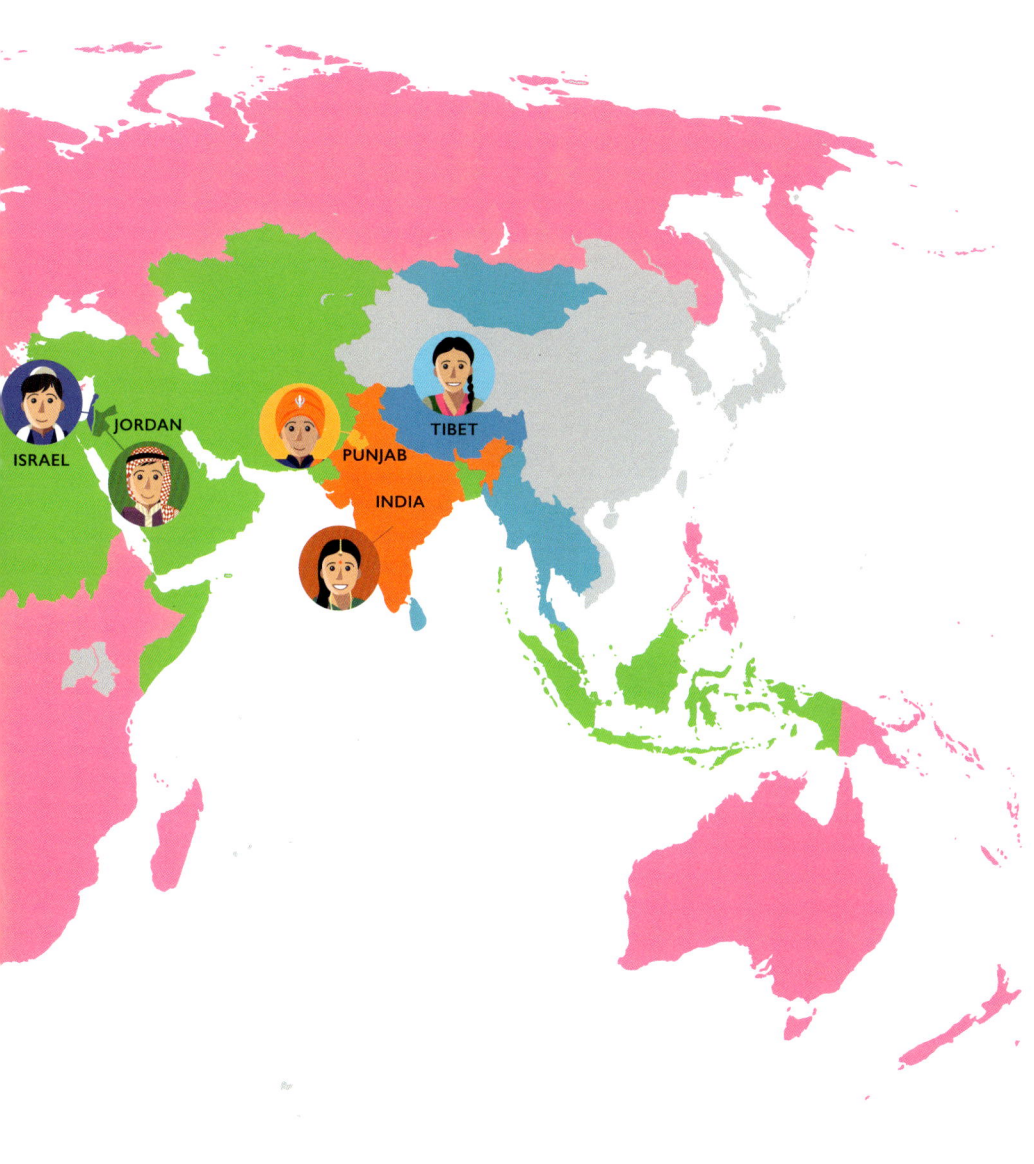

BUDDHISM

Namaskar! That means 'I bow to the divine in you'. We use this greeting because we believe that God exists in everyone we meet.

My name is Nyima, which means 'sun'. I am a Buddhist girl and I live in Tibet which lies north-east of India in the Himalayas, the highest mountains in the world.

I'd like to tell you some things about my religion.

The Beginning

Buddhism was founded about 2,500 years ago in India by a prince called Siddhartha Gautama. The name 'Buddhism' comes from the word 'budhi' which means 'to wake up'. Siddhartha became known as 'The Buddha' which means 'The Awakened One' because he had woken up to the true meaning of life and death. There are over 488 million Buddhists in the world today. China has the most Buddhists, though it has other larger religions.

Prince Siddhartha: The Buddha

Prince Siddhartha was born around 563 BC in the area where Nepal now is. He lived in a city his father ruled. He was a thoughtful, kind person who loved to meditate about life. When he was thirty years old, he left the palace and discovered what life was like in the world outside. He was unhappy when he saw lots of poverty and suffering. Then everything changed for him when he met a very happy monk. He left the royal palace, his parents, his wife and son to become a monk. He travelled around India looking for happiness and peace. He followed a very strict way of life and almost starved to death. He then realised that the right way to happiness was 'The Middle Way', a path between being extremely strict and extremely easy on oneself. Sitting under a fig tree, he suddenly achieved 'Bodhi' which means 'Awakening'. He discovered 'Four Noble Truths' that would help to end suffering in the world. He died, aged eighty, around 483 BC in India.

The Four Noble Truths

1. Suffering is part of life.
2. Wanting things in life causes suffering.
3. Stop wanting things and life's suffering will end.
4. The 'Eightfold Path' will help you to stop wanting things and so end suffering.

We Believe . . .

1. That Buddha was not a god. He was a human being.
2. In a never-ending cycle of birth and death. So, we don't believe in a god who created the universe.
3. In Reincarnation, which is the cycle of living, death and rebirth. We could be reborn as a human, a heavenly being, an animal, a ghost or a resident of hell.
4. In Karma, which means that the quality of our next life depends on how we behave in this life.
5. In Dharma, which is the teaching of the Buddha about the true nature of reality.
6. In the Sangha, which is the community of Buddhists composed of monks, nuns, and ordinary men and women.
7. In the Five Precepts [rules] which tell us how to live good lives.
8. In the Eightfold Path which shows us how to become wiser, happier and more compassionate.
9. In Nirvana which is a perfect state where there is no sense of self any more and you are released from reincarnation.

The Five Precepts [rules] are:

1. Do not harm living things. (However, not all of us are vegetarians.)
2. Do not steal.
3. Love your husband or wife faithfully and respectfully.
4. Do not lie or gossip.
5. Do not drink alcohol or take drugs.

Our Holy Book

The **Tipitaka** is our sacred book, written in an old Indian language called Pali. 'Tipitaka' means 'three baskets' and it has three parts:

1. **The Discipline Basket:** Rules for Buddhist monks and nuns.
2. **The Teaching Basket:** The Buddha's life story.
3. **The Higher Doctrine Basket:** Teachings of the Buddha.

How We Pray

We pray at home or in a temple (a building for prayer). In our homes we have a shrine with incense, candles, pure water and a picture or a statue of the Buddha. But we don't pray to the Buddha. Instead, our prayer is a way of achieving calm and awakening the spiritual strength in us.

Prayer beads, prayer wheels which we spin and mantras help us to reach a peaceful state of mind. A mantra is a word or sound which is repeated over and over to achieve concentration and calm. We also meditate.

Meditation

Meditation is a way of separating yourself from your thoughts and feelings. You reach a state where you are simply being – not thinking but just being aware and at peace.

Here is one type of meditation:

Mindfulness of Breathing: Find a quiet place, sit on the floor with your legs crossed and your back straight. Close your eyes. Concentrate only on your breathing – think of nothing else. With practice your mind will become still and you will experience inner peace.

Our Festivals

1. **Losar:** When Tibetan Buddhists celebrate the New Year.

2. **Buddha Day:** This celebrates the birth and death of the Buddha.

3. **Dharma Day:** This celebrates the first time that the Buddha gave his teachings to the world.

Some Symbols

1. The **Parasol**: protection against evil.
2. The **Golden Fish**: happiness and independence.
3. **The Lotus Flower**: a reminder to overcome all that is bad in the world.
4. The **Conch Shell**: the thoughts of the Buddha
5. The **Dharma Wheel**: knowledge

Marriage

Buddhist marriage is an arrangement between two people or two families and is not a religious event. The Buddha didn't forbid polygamy (having more than one wife) but he advised against it. Separation or divorce is allowed in Buddhism if a couple are unhappy together. In marriage a husband and wife should respect and honour each other.

The Dalai Lama

The **Dalai Lama** is the spiritual leader of Tibetan Buddhists. The name means 'the great guru' – 'guru' meaning 'spiritual teacher'. In 1959, the present Dalai Lama escaped from Tibet after the Chinese army invaded that country and he has lived in India since then. He was awarded the Nobel Peace Prize in 1989 for his non-violent struggle to achieve independence for Tibet. A small boy is chosen to replace the Dalai Lama when he dies. He is considered to be the last Dalai Lama reborn.

There are Buddhist centres in cities and towns all over the world. You are welcome to join us to meditate and achieve calm, even if you don't share our beliefs! I hope you come!

CHRISTIANITY

Dia is Muire duit! My name is Mary and I'm a Christian girl. I live in Ireland. My greeting is in Irish, though we mostly speak English here. It means 'God and Mary be with you!' Mary was the mother of Jesus and I am named after her.

My religion is the largest in the world, about 2.4 billion people – probably because Jesus instructed his followers to take his message to all nations.

We are called 'Christians' because after his death Jesus was given the title 'Christ', meaning 'the anointed one'. (To 'anoint' is to pour sacred oil on a person to show that God has chosen him for a special task.)

I belong to the largest Christian group, the Roman Catholic Church, like most people in my country.

The Beginning

Jesus was born around 2017 years ago in Palestine (roughly where Israel is today). In our calendar, that was Year One. We add AD (Anno Domini = Year of the Lord) and BC (Before Christ) to a date to show whether it came before or after his birth.

Jesus was Jewish, the son of a carpenter. At the age of thirty he began to travel around, preaching to the people. He chose twelve men, mostly fishermen, to be his 'apostles' – his messengers. His message was: 'Love everyone. Do good to those who hate you.' Jesus worked many miracles, helping the blind to see and the lame to walk. Then he was arrested by the Jewish authorities in Jerusalem. They said he claimed to be King of the Jews. The Romans ruled Palestine at that time, so he was taken to the Roman Governor, Pontius Pilate, and condemned to death by crucifixion (nailing him to a cross). After his death, he was resurrected – that is, returned to life. He spoke to his apostles and then ascended into Heaven. The apostles continued to spread his message.

Our Holy Book

Our holy book is the Bible. It is in two parts. The first part is the Old Testament [agreement] which contains some of the holy books of the Jewish people, telling their history and the story of their relationship with God. The second part is the New Testament, containing the Gospels which tell about the life and teachings of Jesus, and the Epistles, which are letters written by his apostles about his teachings.

Types of Christians

The three largest Christian groups are:

1. **The Roman Catholic Church**
   The Pope is its head and lives in the Vatican City in Rome, Italy. Priests serve each Catholic community. They are not allowed to marry. Some men become monks, living in monasteries to pray and do good works. Women cannot become priests. Instead they become nuns and pray, work in the community or are missionaries who go abroad to spread Christianity.

2. **Protestant Churches**
   At the 'Reformation' in 1517, a German monk, Martin Luther, 'protested' against the Catholic Church, saying it had strayed from the teachings of Jesus. The Pope excommunicated him (expelled him from the Church). So he started a new Christian religion, Lutheranism. Afterwards, many other 'Protestant' religions were formed.

3. **Orthodox** ['right belief'] **Churches**
   The Orthodox Churches separated from the Catholic Church centuries ago. They are in East Africa, the Middle East and eastern Europe.

What We Believe

Most types of Christians believe that:

1. There is only one God but there are three persons in God: God the Father (the Creator), God the Son (Jesus) and God the Holy Spirit.
2. God made the universe.
3. Jesus was both God and human.
4. Jesus was the 'Messiah', the saviour sent by God to save people from sin.
5. Jesus rose from the dead.
6. After death we go to God in Heaven or to Hell, depending on whether our lives were good or sinful. Catholics also believe in Purgatory, where people go for a while to get rid of less serious sins.

The Ten Commandments

We follow the same Ten Commandments as Jews do, which were given by God to Moses, as told in the Bible.

1. I am your God.
2. You must not worship false gods.
3. Always say God's name with respect.
4. Keep the Sabbath Day holy (the seventh day of the week: for us, Sunday).
5. Respect your parents.
6. Do not murder.
7. Be faithful to your husband or wife.
8. Do not steal.
9. Do not lie about others.
10. Do not be envious of what others have.

How We Pray

We pray in churches, in our homes, or wherever we are. Catholics must attend church every Sunday. In church we have readings from the Bible, music, song, and sermons on right living. Men and women pray together.

Some Catholics say the Rosary – repeated prayers counted off on 'rosary beads'.

Saints are holy people 'canonized' after death by the Catholic Church. Catholics pray to them and to Mary, Mother of Jesus, asking them to speak to God for them. Protestants do not.

Some of Our Ceremonies (called Sacraments)

1. **Baptism:** To become Christians, water is poured over babies' foreheads as a sign of sin being washed away. Adults are also baptised if they want to become Christians.
2. **The Eucharist ('Holy Communion'):** At the Last Supper before he died, Jesus gave bread to his apostles and shared wine with them. He asked them to do this in his memory. Catholics do this at Mass, believing that Jesus is actually present in the bread and wine, though usually they share only the bread and not the wine.
4. **Marriage:** Husband and wife promise to love and honour each other. We have only one marriage partner, for life.
5. **Penance:** We confess our sins to a priest and receive the forgiveness of God.

Symbols

The Cross reminds us of Jesus's crucifixion; **The Dove** is a symbol of the Holy Spirit; **The Candle** represents Jesus who said: 'I am the Light of the World.'

Festivals

Our most important festivals are Christmas and Easter.

1. Christmas celebrates the birth of Jesus. We have big family dinners and give gifts, especially to the children.
2. In the weeks leading up to Easter (called Lent) we give up things like sweets or alcohol, remembering how Jesus fasted for 40 days in the desert before he began his teaching. On Good Friday we mourn the death of Jesus. Then on Easter Sunday we celebrate his resurrection.

Jesus's message was one of peace and love. I think it is sad that even Christians still continue to make war today!

 # HINDUISM

Namaste! My name is Alisha and I live in India. My greeting in Hindi means "I bow to the divine in you", because we believe that God is present in everyone. So, whenever I greet you, I bow my head and press my hands together in front of my chest.

The Beginning

Hinduism is the world's third largest religion, with over one billion Hindus in the world today! 80% of the people of India are Hindus. It is one of the oldest religions in the world, about 4,000 years old. Unlike other major religions, it wasn't founded by any one person.

Hindu Gods

We have many gods and goddesses but each stands for a different form of our one supreme, eternal spirit Brahman who is present in all things. We do not worship Brahman – instead we choose one of the other gods to worship. My favourite is Krishna who is often shown as a beautiful young man playing a flute. He stands for love, human and divine. Other people prefer gods like Durga the Mother Goddess or Ganesh, the elephant-headed god of wisdom who removes obstacles in our lives.

Brahma, **Vishnu** and **Shiva** are the most important forms of Brahman. Brahma created the universe. Vishnu protects humans and keeps order in the world. Shiva destroys and brings change so that things can be reborn.

There are many other gods, like **Hanuman**, the monkey god of strength and devotion, and **Kali**, goddess of death, time and doomsday.

We Believe . . .

1. In a supreme spirit, Brahman, who is present in all things in the universe.
2. That each of us has an inner self or soul.
3. In Reincarnation – that after we die we are reborn and this continues until we become perfect and are one with Brahman.
4. In Karma – that the quality of our next life depends on how we behave in this life.
5. In Dharma, which is a right way of living for each person that supports positive order in the universe. (For Buddhists 'Dharma' means something different.)

The Five Hindu Practices are: Daily worship; Following Dharma; Celebrating Holy Days; Going on pilgrimages; Cremation: we burn our dead on a pile of sandalwood logs.

The Caste System

Each Hindu is born into a group of people called a 'caste'. There are four.
1. **Brahims:** Scholars, priests, judges, landowners and teachers.
2. **Kshatriyas:** Warriors, fighters and rulers.
3. **Vaishyas:** Farmers, traders, shopkeepers, moneylenders and merchants.
4. **Sudras:** Unskilled workers.

There are also the **Dalit** who are outside the caste system. They do all the dirty work and other Hindus are not supposed to touch them. They are fighting for their rights now in the modern world.

Our Holy Books

The Vedas tell us about our beliefs and ceremonies. They are written in Sanskrit, the most sacred language of Hinduism.

The Upanishads are sacred texts written between 500 to 1000 years after the Vedas. They tell us about Hinduism.

The Bhagavad-Gita *[Song of the Lord]* is an ancient text and the world's longest poem! It teaches us how to gain perfect self-knowledge and be happy.

The Ramayana is a story. Princess Sita is kidnapped and her husband Prince Rama sets out to rescue her. After years they are reunited and return home to find the streets decorated with flowers and lamps to celebrate their safe return.

How We Pray

We pray at home and in our temples which honour different gods.

We can start our day by chanting the prayer 'O Mother Earth'. The best times to worship are at dawn and at dusk when everything is quiet and peaceful.

Yoga

Many of us practise yoga, which began in ancient India. It helps us physically, mentally and spiritually. It has now spread all over the world and millions of non-Hindu people practise it.

'Aum' or 'Om'

This sacred sound is a chant to meditate on God. It is also a sacred symbol. There are three syllables – a, u and m – so it is pronounced 'Ah-oo-mm'.

Our Festivals

Diwali, the Festival of Light, is in the Hindu month of Kartik (October or November). We celebrate the victory of light over darkness and good over evil. We light up the streets with thousands of oil lamps, lanterns, candles, let off fireworks, visit our relatives and have parties where we share sweets and dried fruit, and give presents to the poor.

Holi or 'Festival of Colours' is a two-day festival that celebrates the arrival of springtime.

Janmashtami celebrates the birthday of our favourite god 'Lord Krishna'.

Navaratri celebrates our Mother Goddess Durga. Some Hindus fast during the nine nights to honour Durga.

Guru Purnima means 'Teachers' Full Moon' and is in the Hindu month of Ashadha (June or July). We pay respect to our Gurus who give us knowledge and teach us right from wrong.

Our Food and Drink

It is forbidden to us to kill a cow or eat beef. Cows wander freely around the countryside, streets and towns. It is good luck to give food to a cow! Many of us are vegetarians and dairy products are very popular. We use spices to add flavour to our food and we eat lots of curry, rice and flatbread like naan bread and chapatis.

Our Pilgrimages

We make at least one pilgrimage in our lifetime. Here are a few:

1. **The River Ganges:** This is the holiest river for us. We go there to wash away our sins. The ashes of cremated Hindus are often spread across the water.
2. **Kumbh Mela;** At this time 40 million Hindus bathe in the holy waters at the meeting of the rivers Jumna and Ganges. We believe that this washes our sins away and our spirits are cleansed.
3. **Varanasi:** This city on the Ganges is the home of the god Shiva. If we die there and have our ashes scattered on the river, we have achieved the best death possible.

I hope you can attend one of our wonderful pilgrimages or festivals one day!

ISLAM

As-salamu alaikum! Peace be to you! My name is Rachid and I am a Muslim boy. I live in Jordan. Our language is Arabic which is also the official language of 27 other Muslim countries.

Islam

The word 'Islam' means 'submission to the will of God'. Islam is over 1,400 years old. It began in Mecca in Arabia in 610 AD. Islam is the second-largest religion in the world with over 1.6 billion believers. Followers of Islam are called Muslims. The founder of Islam was the Prophet Muhammad, peace be upon him. We have great respect for our prophets (those chosen to speak for Allah) and we always add 'peace be upon him' when we say one of their names. When we write in English this becomes 'pbuh' for short.

The Arabic word for the one and only God is 'Allah'. Muslims consider it disrespectful to draw or paint a picture of Allah or Muhammad (pbuh).

Muhammad

Muhammad (pbuh) was born in Mecca, Saudi Arabia, in 570 AD. He was a merchant who liked to pray alone in a cave near Mecca. When he was forty years old the Angel Jibril (Gabriel) appeared in the cave and recited the words of Allah to him. He told Muhammad (pbuh) that he was the last prophet that would be sent by Allah. We remember his life, sayings and stories to help us to be good Muslims. He died when he was 63, in 632 AD, in Medina, Saudi Arabia.

Our Holy Book

Our Holy Book is called the Quran. It contains the word of Allah which the Angel Jibril (Gabriel) recited to Muhammad (pbuh). Later these revelations were written down in Arabic. We believe that it is Allah's final and sacred word. It teaches us how to live a good life and how to worship.

The Five Pillars of Islam

1. Saying: 'There is no god except Allah and Muhammad is the messenger of Allah.'
2. Praying at five special times every day.
3. Giving money to the poor.
4. Fasting during Ramadan.
5. Going on a pilgrimage to Mecca at least once in our lives if we can.

How We Pray

We pray facing in the direction of Mecca, the birthplace of Muhammad (pbuh). We pray five times a day: at dawn, midday, afternoon, after sunset and at night. We pray wherever we are at the times for prayer.

On Fridays a man called a 'muezzin' calls us to prayer from the minaret [tower] on top of the mosque. We take off our shoes when we enter the mosque and wash our feet. We kneel on a prayer mat. We stand, bow and kneel when we pray. An 'imam' stands on a raised platform to lead the people in prayer. He is a Quran expert. There are no pictures or statues in mosques but some have walls decorated with verses from the Quran. Women and children pray apart from the men in the mosque.

The three most important mosques in the world are the Grand Mosque in Mecca, Muhammad's (pbuh) Mosque in Medina, and the Al-Aqsa Mosque in Jerusalem.

Our Holy City

Mecca is the holiest city in Islam. The cube-shaped Holy Kaaba or 'House of God' is in the centre of our most sacred mosque, the Grand Mosque. Muslims, if they are able, are expected to visit Mecca at least once in their lifetime. This pilgrimage is called the 'Hajj' and takes place every year.

Our Food & Drink

The Quran tells us:

1. Not to eat pork.
2. Not to drink alcohol. (Alcohol is banned from some Islamic countries.)
3. Not to eat or drink from sunrise to sunset during Ramadan.
4. To eat only 'halal' meat. This means that the animal is killed in a special way and prayed over.

Our Symbols

1. **The Star and Crescent**
   Our best-known symbol is the 'Star and Crescent' [crescent moon]. Some Muslim countries including Turkey, Algeria, and Pakistan have it on their flags.
2. **'Allah' in Arabic**
   The word 'Allah' written in Arabic script can represent Islam.

Our Festivals

1. **Ramadan** begins with the sighting of a new moon, marking the start of the ninth month in the Islamic calendar. It is our holiest month. Every day we fast from dawn till dusk, not even drinking water. We read the Quran, we pray and we give to charity.
2. **Eid al-Fitr** [Festival of Breaking the Fast] marks the end of Ramadan. It lasts for three days. We celebrate, give money to the poor and presents to the children.
3. **Eid al-Adha** [Feast of the Sacrifice] celebrates the event in the Quran when the Prophet Ibrahim [Abraham] (pbuh) is about to sacrifice his son on God's command, but then God gives him a ram to sacrifice instead. It comes at the end of the Hajj, the pilgrimage to Mecca.

4. **Al-Hijra** celebrates the beginning of the Islamic New Year. It is celebrated on the first day of Muharram, the month in which Muhammad (pbuh) emigrated from Mecca to Medina in 622 AD (the Hijra). Islamic years are calculated from 1 Muharram, 622 AD.

Marriage

Marriage is very important for Muslims. A Muslim man can have more than one wife at the same time, up to a total of four. This is called polygamy. However, a Muslim woman can only have one husband.

Women in Islam

Muslim women are expected to be very modest. They must always keep themselves covered up, with their hair covered with a scarf called a hijab. Sometimes they wear a niqab which is a veil covering the face except the eyes, and in some countries a burka which covers the whole body with just a mesh to see through.

In some Muslim countries women are not allowed any contact with men outside their families and every woman must have a male guardian who must give them permission to travel or get married and so on. Some women are fighting to get their rights and have just won the right to drive a car in Saudi Arabia.

Muslims, Jews and Christians have a lot in common. We honour the same prophets, like Ibrahim [Abraham] (pbuh) and Musa [Moses] (pbuh). Isa [Jesus] (pbuh) is one of our prophets too. So I think we should all live in peace.

JUDAISM

Shalom! That greeting means 'Peace!' My name is Jacob and I am a Jewish boy. I live in Jerusalem, the capital of Israel.

Being a Jew is not just a matter of belonging to the Jewish religion – it also means belonging to a particular 'ethnic group' – that is, a large group of people who share the same origins, language and culture.

Our language in Israel, Hebrew, is a very ancient one. Yiddish in another language spoken by many Jews worldwide.

There are only 6.5 million Jews in our country, Israel, but over 14 million Jews altogether in the world today.

The Name of God

In our ancient holy books, God was referred to as 'YHWH' as they didn't write down his true name, out of respect. It is pronounced 'Yahweh'. Nowadays we refer to Him as 'My Lord' or 'The Name'. Here, in English, I will just say 'God'.

The Beginning

Our religion began around 2000 BC in the Middle East, with a 'covenant' (agreement) which God made with a Hebrew called Abraham. The names 'Hebrews', 'Israelites' and 'Jews' are all used to describe the descendants of Abraham. God told Abraham to leave his home in Mesopotamia and travel with his wife Sarah to a different country. He promised him land and lots of descendants. Abraham agreed.

Moses is also an important figure in our history. He grew up as an Egyptian prince but he was actually the son of a Hebrew slave. God helped him to free the Hebrews from slavery in Egypt. After forty years wandering in the Sinai desert, they came to the 'Promised Land' which is roughly where my country Israel is today.

Moses received the Ten Commandments from God on Mount Sinai.

Christians follow the same Ten Commandments as we do, because one of our Holy Books is also theirs. This is because Jesus, who founded their religion, was a Jew.

The Ten Commandments

1. I am your God.
2. You must not worship false gods.
3. Always say God's name with respect.
4. Honour God by resting on the Sabbath day (the seventh day of the week: for us, Saturday).
5. Respect your parents.
6. Do not murder.
7. Be faithful to your husband or wife.
8. Do not steal.
9. Do not lie about others.
10. Do not be envious of what others have.

Our Holy Books

The Tanakh and the Torah

The Tanakh tells the history of the Jewish people and their relationship to God. It is written in Hebrew and contains the 'Torah' which are the books of the Prophet Moses, together with those of other prophets and other writings. (A prophet is one chosen to speak for God.)

The 'Torah' scrolls are kept in an 'Ark', a holy cabinet in each synagogue (the building where we pray). It is our holiest book, so holy it cannot be touched by hand.

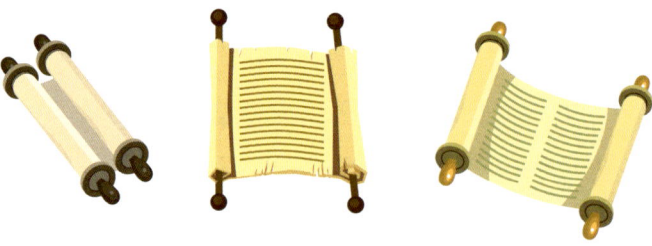

The Talmud

The Talmud is over 6,200 pages long! It is a collection of law, legend, philosophy, history, science and humour. It is written in Hebrew and in Aramaic (another language spoken by the Jews in ancient times).

Where We Pray

The Synagogue

On Saturday, the Sabbath, we go to a synagogue to pray and learn about God. We rest on that day as God rested on the seventh day after creating the world. We also go to the synagogue for all our ceremonies.

When praying, men and boys wear a skullcap called a kippah (or yarmulke) and a prayer shawl called a tallit. Some wear the kippah all the time.

Our Rabbi

An important member of our community is our rabbi. He is a 'Torah' expert, helping us to understand our religion better. He leads us in celebrations and at funerals.

Our Food

We only eat 'kosher' [proper] food which means food approved of by our religion. We eat only certain kinds of meat and fish – for example, we do not eat pork or shellfish. Only animals slaughtered by a specially trained Jewish person, by a single swift cut across the throat, are kosher. Also, we drain all the blood from meat before it can be eaten. Fruits and vegetables are kosher. We eat dairy products but we never eat dairy products and meat at the same meal. Our laws on food are quite tricky!

Symbols

1. **Star of David:** A six-pointed star which is on the national flag of Israel.
2. **Menorah:** A seven-branched candelabra reminding us that God made the world in seven days.
3. **Mezuzah:** A small case holding a tiny scroll with verses from the Torah and fixed to the doorposts of our homes. It is touched when entering and leaving.
4. **Shofar:** A trumpet made from a ram's horn and blown every day during the month before the beginning of the Jewish New Year.

Bar Mitzvah/Bat Mitzvah

'Mitzvah' means 'commandment' in Hebrew. 'Bar Mitzvah' means 'Son of the Commandment' and 'Bat Mitzvah' means 'Daughter of the Commandment'. At age 13, a boy's Bar Mitzvah is celebrated and at 12 a girl's Bat Mitzvah. They are then considered to be responsible adult Jews, knowing right from wrong.

Our Festivals

1. **Yom Kippur** *[Day of Atonement]* is the holiest day in the Jewish year. We fast and take no drink, to make up for any wrong things we have done.
2. **Passover:** Held in the springtime, it lasts for eight days. It reminds us that God helped our ancestors to escape from Egyptian slavery.
3. **Rosh Hashanah** *[Feast of the Trumpets]* celebrates the Jewish New Year. *Shanah Tovah!* – Have a good year!
4. **Hanukkah** *[Festival of Lights]* is celebrated in December. We give presents to each other and children are given gifts of money!

Different Types of Judaism

Some types of Judaism are more strict than others. Orthodox Judaism is very strict, Reform Judaism is more modern-thinking, and Conservative Judaism is in between.

Women in Judaism

Women are strong figures in our families and communities. Traditionally, a child is Jewish only if its mother is – not if its father is. However, in synagogues women stay on a balcony, separate from the men. They can't become rabbis or even read from the holy books in synagogue. Now things are changing, however, in Reform Judaism.

The Holocaust

During World War II six million European Jews were murdered in gas chambers by Adolf Hitler's Nazi Germany. More than 1.5 million children from across Europe died during the dark days of the Holocaust.

I hope you visit my country Israel someday – and see our wonderful capital Jerusalem which is a holy city for Jews, Muslims and Christians!

SIKHISM

Sat Sri Akal! That means 'God is Truth' and it is how Sikhs greet each other. My name is Aashish and I'm a Sikh. I live in the Punjab, an area in northern India which stretches into northern Pakistan. I think my religion is very special in many ways and I'd love to tell you all about it.

The Beginning

Sikhism is the ninth largest world religion, with about 28 million followers. It is quite a new religion as it was founded only about 520 years ago. That's young for a religion! The word 'Sikh' means 'seeker of truth'. Our religion is based on the teachings of Guru Nanak and the nine gurus who followed after him. The title 'Guru' means 'spiritual leader'. There are no living gurus now and our holy book, Guru Granth Sahib, is our only teacher.

Guru Nanak

Guru Nanak was born in 1469 AD in the Punjab, to Hindu parents. He was always very interested in religion and meditation. He was married and had two sons. When he was twenty-eight years old he went down to a river to bathe and meditate. He didn't return for three days! Then, filled with God's spirit, he began to tell the world about Sikhism. He travelled throughout India, Arabia and Persia, spreading his message of kindness and peace. He died in 1539 AD.

Our Holy Book

Our Holy Book, Guru Granth Sahib, is a collection of teachings that Guru Nanak, the other Gurus, and Sikh, Muslim and Hindu saints have left us. Written in Punjabi, it is read during every Sikh festival. It contains 5894 hymns and religious poems.

We Believe . . .

1. In one God who has many names: God, Allah, Yahweh and so on. All religions lead us to the same God.
2. We are all equal – all children of God.
3. Men and women are equal.
4. Animals too have souls.
5. In Reincarnation: that when we die we will be born again either as humans or animals. We continue to be reborn into this world until we become perfect and then we become one with God.
6. We should be truthful, hardworking, humble and loving.
7. We must share our wealth with the needy.

How We Pray

We pray at home and in a special building called the Gurdwara, whose name means 'doorway to the Guru'. Flags called Nishan Sahib on tall poles fly outside with our special 'khanda' symbol on them. Inside, having removed our shoes, we wash our hands and feet. We sit on the floor, side by side. There are no special seats as we are all of equal importance, rich and poor. We usually leave food or money as offerings. We have no statues or religious pictures in the Gurdwara. Our Holy Book is placed on a lectern on a raised platform. The holiest Gurdwara is the 'Golden Temple' in the city of Amristar in the Punjab, India. Our temple is used for the singing of hymns and readings from the Holy Book. It has libraries of Sikh scriptures and schools where children learn the scriptures. It is also used for 'Langar' which are free vegetarian meals served to anyone who comes. All are welcome in our Gurdwaras, even those who have no faith at all.

The Five Ks

We wear the 'Five Ks', showing that we are dedicated to a life of devotion and obedience to the Guru. These are:

1. **Kesh:** Uncut hair as a sign of holiness and obedience to God.
2. **Kangha:** A comb in our hair as a sign of cleanliness. We wear a turban to keep our hair tidy. Women wear scarves but some wear a turban.
3. **Kara:** A steel bracelet on our left wrists symbolising that God is everlasting.
4. **Kachera:** Cotton underwear shorts as a sign of our dignity and modesty.
5. **Kirpan:** A short dagger, to remind us that we must protect those who are weak and defenceless. It's never to be used in anger.

Our Ceremonies

Marriage

Sikh marriages take place in a Gurdwara. Some weddings are arranged by parents. During the ceremony, the bride and groom walk four times around the Holy Book. Being faithful to one husband or wife is the rule and we believe you are not complete without a spouse (husband or wife) by your side.

Funerals

Upon dying, a Sikh's body is washed and dressed in traditional Sikh clothes. It is taken to the Gurdwara and placed in front of the Holy Book. We believe that death is simply a small sleep before rebirth. We cremate the dead person on a pyre of wood which is lit by a close relative. The ashes are collected and are scattered in the sea, in running water or buried in the ground.

Our Symbols

Our symbols are very important to us.

Among them are:

1. **Khanda**
   This symbol is of a double-edged sword representing our belief in one God. The Chakar is a circle around the Khanda, reminding us that God has no beginning and no end. There are two crossed swords called Kirpans around the Chakar which remind us of our duty to God and to society.

2. **Ik Onkar**
   This means 'One with Everything'. These words are often found in homes and in Gurdwaras, decorating the walls.

Our Women

Men and women in our religion are equal. Sikh women read scripture, conduct services, lead prayers in the Gurdwara and are called the 'mothers of mankind'.

Our Festivals

1. **Vaisakhi:** Our biggest festival celebrates the harvest and the Sikh New Year in April.
2. **Guru Nanak:** This celebrates Guru Nanak's birthday in November.
3. **Diwali:** This 'Festival of Lights' celebrates the victory of light over darkness and good over evil. It lasts for five days in autumn and is a time for the giving of gifts.

I hope you can come to one of our festivals someday or visit one of our temples to share a 'Langar' free meal. You're very welcome!

If you enjoyed this book from Poolbeg why not grab your next page-turner?

www.poolbeg.com

FAST DELIVERY – All books despatched within 24 hours

FREE DELIVERY – on orders in Rep. of Ireland!*

Whether it's for you or a friend, we've got your next story waiting.

Exclusive offers, new releases – and more from poolbeg.com

FOLLOW US ON SOCIAL MEDIA:

X @PoolbegBooks
 @poolbegbooks
 facebook.com/poolbegpress

*Free delivery in Rep. of Ireland. See our website above for details.